"I DIDN'T DO IT"

"I didn't do it"

DEALING WITH DISHONESTY

Elaine K. McEwan

Harold Shaw Publishers
Wheaton, Illinois

All Scripture quotations, unless otherwise indicated, are taken from *The Holy Bible: New International Version.* Copyright © 1973, 1978, 1984 by the International Bible Society. Used by permission of Zondervan Publishing House.

Cover design by David LaPlaca

Edited by Joan Guest

ISBN 0-87788-177-4

Library of Congress Cataloging-in-Publication Data

McEwan, Elaine K., 1941-
I didn't do it: dealing with dishonesty / by Elaine K. McEwan.
p. cm.
Includes bibliographical references.
ISBN 0-87788-177-4
1.
CIP

---

03 02 01 00 99 98 97 96

10 9 8 7 6 5 4 3 2 1

Contents

1

Is It Normal to Be Dishonest?

My husband, a Native American Chicka-hominy from the tidewater area of Virginia, grew up in a large and fun-loving family (nine siblings). They love to relate anecdotes about their growing-up years, and one favorite is titled "The Cap Pistol." My husband, Raymond, is the featured character. When he was a boy of seven or eight, his mother was bent on teaching him the lessons of caring and sharing.

Each day when he returned from the one-room school where he and twenty or more siblings and cousins attended, he walked through the forest to the home of an elderly woman who was ill. He brought in wood for her cookstove, carried water in buckets from the spring, and fetched groceries from the small general store. Each day she gave him two shiny pennies for his services, much to his mother's dismay, for she had wanted him to learn about helping and serving those in need. But the neighbor insisted, and so young Raymond used his pennies to purchase candy treats, like "Mary Janes."

After several weeks of indulging his sweet tooth, Mumma Adkins decided that a new lesson must be learned: frugality. Now she insisted that, instead of spending his hard-earned pennies, he deposit them in a jar kept on the kitchen counter.

As Christmas neared, the general store received a shipment of shiny cap pistols. They were tantalizing to young Raymond. He knew the likelihood of someone purchasing one for him for Christmas was almost non-existent. Christmas presents were by necessity more practical. But, he theorized, perhaps he could make a withdrawal from his savings account and purchase one for himself. One day when Mumma was out of the kitchen, he climbed up on the counter and began counting out the needed amount.

Alas, however, his savings withdrawal was interrupted when Mumma walked into the room. But quick-witted Raymond managed to convince his mother that he was making the withdrawal to purchase a Christmas gift for someone. Of course, he could not tell her for whom he was buying this present. She smiled, certain for whom the present was intended, and permitted him to count out the required pennies.

After he had made his purchase, Raymond realized his moral dilemma. He'd told his mother he was purchasing a gift for someone else. Now what was he to do? Once again, his quick wits came to the rescue. He would wrap up the cap pistol and give it to his parents for Christmas. Perhaps they would generously share it with him. As the family gathered around the pot-bellied stove that dominated the living area of their small home, he waited with eager anticipation for his mother to open the gift.

She burst into laughter when she unwrapped the pistol, immediately recalling the circumstances of its purchase. "Well," she mused, "I can just see Papa and me fighting over who will get to play with this." Young Raymond was permitted to use the cap pistol only until the caps that came with it were expended, and then the gun disappeared. He was wise enough not to ask where it had gone. He knew it wasn't really his.

When Mumma Adkins died at the age of eighty-three, the cap pistol was found among her things. Kept in a box of treasured objects and memorabilia, it had obviously been part of a cherished memory for more than fifty years. Today's self-indulgent parents (myself among them) would no doubt have given the cap pistol to our clever and creative child. But Mumma Adkins had a lesson to teach young Raymond, albeit a quiet and gentle one. The lesson still lives on today. Although the cap pistol now has a place of honor among my treasured objects, it has never been fired since Mother Adkins put it away so many decades ago. Raymond has the explanation—"My mother wouldn't approve."

My husband's twelve grandchildren delight in hearing the story, and guests to our home are enchanted as they examine the nearly antique toy. But most important are the lessons of honesty that Mumma Adkins so skillfully and subtly taught. They live on in the integrity of her children and grandchildren.

Regardless of the generation, parents want their children to be honest. In yearly studies conducted by

9

the National Research Center at the University of Chicago between 1972 and 1986, honesty consistently showed up as the single most desirable quality for a child to have. Parents considered it even more important than being a good student.

But somehow, the old-fashioned virtues and moral absolutes that were givens in nearly every family of bygone generations have been lost to thousands of current parents. Witness the proliferation of self-help and parenting books (mine included) purporting to help parents to more effectively model and teach the virtues and values of honesty, respect, and trustworthiness. Qualities that used to be taken for granted as part of every child's upbringing lost their favor among the generation that wanted freedom and the opportunity to "do its own thing."

A recent survey compiled by the Josephson Institute of Ethics and reported in USA Today[1] found "an absolute erosion of the American character." The nonprofit group's 1996 report—a three-year survey of eleven thousand high schoolers, college students, and adults—found that dishonesty had worsened since its 1993 survey. Among the significant findings:

- 37 percent of high schoolers say they stole from a store in the past twelve months, up from 33 percent in 1993; 65 percent cheated on an exam, up from 61 percent.
- 17 percent of collegiate respondents say they stole in the past year, up from 16 percent in 1993; 24 percent say they would lie to get or keep a job, up from 21 percent.

Other findings show that the young take cues from adults. For instance, 47 percent of adults say they would probably accept an auto body repairman's offer to include unrelated damages in an insurance claim.

The number of cheaters is probably higher, reports Josephson: 34 percent say they gave at least one dishonest answer.

When I was an elementary school principal, dishonest students were among my most challenging disciplinary problems. Unfortunately, I had to deal with lying, cheating, and stealing almost every day of the week. My aim was not merely to "catch the culprits" and mete out punishment. My most important goals were helping parents to recognize the serious nature of their child's dishonesty, and helping children learn from their mistakes and move on.

The biblical principles of confession, repentance, restitution, and forgiveness were never labeled as such, but I definitely made them a part of the process of restoration for each child who had a problem with dishonesty in my school. I always threw in a teaching lesson or two as well—the kind that many children weren't getting at home on a regular basis. Although I was an administrator in a public school, I made no apologies for the biblical standards of honesty that were expectations in my school.

Unfortunately, the school setting, much like the real world, seems to offer children multiple opportunities for dishonesty. One study showed that 22 percent of students begin to cheat in the first grade and by eighth grade, 49 percent of children admit they have cheated on school assignments. A survey of high school students in California revealed that three-quarters of them cheated on exams. Thirty percent of college freshmen say they cheated on a test in their last year of high school.[2] Does this widespread admission of cheating represent a moral decline or just normal behavior from kids who were given too little supervision and too much opportunity? Probably a little of both.

Isn't dishonesty a normal part of growing up?

Matthew was just six years old, a charming and precocious first grader. He was accused of flushing Jonathan's mittens down the toilet. There were several witnesses to this dastardly deed, but Matthew assured me that he couldn't have done it. He lied (and quite impressively, I might add). Without the credible witnesses, I might easily have been persuaded by his guileless assurances.

Those who think young children are too innocent to lie just haven't spent much time with them. My friend Kim reports that even her preschooler, when confronted with an empty popsicle box and the evidence still dripping from his chin, denied that he had polished off what was left in the box.

There are several studies suggesting that children can lie at a much earlier age than most adults would think and actually can be quite sophisticated in their decision making regarding the lies.

One researcher tempted preschool children to lie to protect someone they liked from punishment. Children were left in a room with a toy and told not to play with it. When an adult joined them and played with the toy and broke it, they were then questioned about who had done it. Of those children who knew the adult well, nearly half did not inform on the adult. Among the children who did not know the adult, all of them told the truth and informed on the adult stranger.[3]

It happens even in the best of families. Our kids are human, just like we are. There are lots of reasons kids lie, cheat, and steal, many of them pretty understandable. On the one hand, you have to admire the preschoolers who had developed enough loyalty to an adult to want to protect them from punishment, even if they were lying. Chapter 2 will help you understand some of the more common reasons for dishonesty in children. With understanding comes the ability to respond in the positive and loving ways that will help your child become the honest person you want her to become.

Minor incidents of stealing, lying, and cheating occur frequently in early childhood. Just because your son took a candy bar from the local convenience store doesn't mean he's destined for the penitentary when he graduates from high school. It's not the end of the world when your daughter copies the answers from a friend on the math test. Neither can you afford to dismiss such occurrences as "all part of growing up." The quality of our parental response can well set the tone for the future in terms of our children's honesty and integrity.

Chapter 3 gives suggestions on how to handle specific episodes of cheating, stealing, and lying when they occur in your family. It takes time and lots of parental guidance for children to develop their own well-integrated sense of honesty, so don't expect your child to emerge as a paragon of virtue overnight.

Chapter 4 provides dozens of ways to regularly teach and encourage honesty in your children. If regular episodes of dishonesty occur after the age of ten, it's time for serious interventions and immediate professional assistance.

Can you predict which kids will be honest and which won't?

Researchers have looked at honesty in many different ways in an attempt to determine its relationship to other characteristics like age, sex, and intelligence. They have discovered some interesting things but no specific clear-cut answers as to why some kids have problems with lying, cheating, and stealing and others don't. There's no difference between boys and girls with regard to their honesty.

Intelligence, academic ability, and achievement are positively correlated with honesty. According to a landmark study done by Hartshorne and May, smarter children lie less.[4] This could be because the intelligent child recognizes the risks associated with dishonesty, or it could also be that his intelligence gives him the tools to reach his goals without being dishonest. Dishonesty is often part of a pattern of manipulation seen in some children; sometimes dishonesty is associated with lack of parental supervision; and sometimes dishonesty seems to happen when kids get mixed up with the wrong crowd. Some kids who lie the most come from homes in which parents also lie often or endorse breaking rules, but this is certainly not always the case.[5]

So, making predictions about children and their propensity for honesty based on some characteristic in their background, personality, or home situation is dubious at best and downright dangerous at worst.

What are the stages of moral development?

Children are not born as morally developed human beings. They pass through various developmental stages, hence the need for constant teaching and guidance along the way. But they are far more capable of responding to our nurturing and making wise moral choices than many popular theorists would suggest. Beware of writings by theorists who believe we shouldn't expect too much from young children because they just aren't capable of making moral decisions before they have passed through certain stages. I recommend the approach of Schulman and Mekler, who suggest three phases of moral development.[6]

During the first phase, children are internalizing the parental standards of right and wrong action. Your approach to discipline and teaching during this stage is particularly important, since children internalize the standards of loving parents much more readily than those of cold or abusive parents.[7]

During the second phase, children are learning to develop empathic reactions to other people's feelings; they are beginning to be able to feel the pain and joy of others. Children need to be able to feel good when they do nice things for others and feel guilt when they hurt others. There are many activities in which parents can engage to help children of all ages develop empathy, a critical attribute for the development of honesty. A child who cannot answer the questions "How will your friend feel if you take his bicycle without asking?" or "How will the teacher feel if you copy the answers from someone else?" is one who has not yet developed empathy.

The final phase is one of constructing personal standards of right and wrong. The child or young adult in this phase is now able to reason about the long-term effects of her actions.

What are the biggest mistakes parents make in trying to bring up children with a sense of honesty?

It's easy to go astray when trying to help your children develop a sense of honesty. Here are some of the little mistakes in judgment that parents sometimes make along the way which can often result in big problems.

Some parents think that their little cherubs are *naturally good but become morally corrupted* when exposed to the wrong social and cultural influences. So, they conclude, if they can just keep them away from anything that's bad (television, friends, books, movies), the kids will be fine. In the first place, you can't protect your kids from everything; eventually they'll be exposed to corruption, and without a well-developed set of internal personal moral standards, they'll be seriously adrift. In the second place, taking a proactive stance which encourages and nurtures moral development will be much more successful than the negative, repressive stance which is always preaching and saying no.

Another group of parents believes that their children have been *delivered to them with predominantly immoral* tendencies and that moral sensibilities must be imposed upon them from the outside, against their will. While I certainly believe in original sin and know that without God we have no hope of redemption, I also believe that approaching child-rearing like an itinerant evangelist preaching hellfire and brimstone will do little to help your children internalize the moral values you wish to instill. You may well send them straight into the arms of disaster because they will internalize God's wrath.

There is still another group that believes parents and *parents alone are not only accountable but completely responsible* for their child's moral character. This belief can set us up for serious disappointment when our children do not make the choices that we know they should make. In his book *Parents in Pain,* Dr. John White cautions parents against taking too much ownership for their children's problems. We hope and pray that they will be honest and ethical in everything they do, but we must remember that ultimately our children are their own persons, and particularly when they reach young adulthood, they are free to make their own decisions and embrace their own values.[8]

Still another mistake that many parents make is believing that there is little they can do about a child's moral character, since the *child's personality is pre-*

destined by genetic factors that are largely beyond any-one's control. These parents approach child-rearing with a permissive, laissez-faire attitude, which is just as deleterious to a child's moral upbringing as being too rigid and punitive. Permissive parents who don't insist that their children live up to moral rules tend to have children who are aggressive, self-centered, and irresponsible.[9]

The final mistake that many of us make is believing that *moral education means preaching* to children about the values and virtues we expect them to ex-emplify. Kids are amazingly bright. They seem to have an uncanny ability to see right through our lectures and pontificating. If our own lives are not models of honesty, we cannot expect that lectures will have any positive effect at all. Walk your talk!

What is honesty?

Most people, when asked to define honesty, will men-tion terms like *trustworthiness, integrity,* and *depend-ability.* There are some who will extend the definition of honesty to being truthful in sharing thoughts and feelings with friends and family. And others would even include in that definition being honest with one-self. But if you quiz children on what it means to be honest, they will define honesty in terms of the Big Three: lying, cheating, and stealing. These are non-violent offenses that involve deceit, sneakiness, con-cealment, misrepresentation, and breach of trust. The media sometimes describes them as "white-collar" crimes.

To define lying, cheating, and stealing may seem unnecessary. But for purposes of discussion in the following chapters, here are my working definitions of the Big Three.

Lying: a deliberate denial or a misrepresentation (e.g., withholding part of the truth in a misleading way) with the intent to deceive another in order to gain an advantage or evade consequences. Lying can take a number of different forms. I've heard them all:

- Simple reversals of truth. "But, Dr. McEwan, I turned in my homework. I don't know what happened to it."
- Exaggerations. "My dad's going to give me a hundred dollars if I get all *As* on my report card."
- Fabrications. "We went to Disney World over Christmas vacation."
- Confabulations (stories that are partly true and partly false). "I didn't get my homework done because my mother said I had to go to church last night."
- Wrong accusations. "Who, me? I didn't break the window. It was Johnny who did it."

Cheating: a combination of lying and stealing with intent to misrepresent knowledge or skill; deception or fraud that involves taking advantage of another person.

Stealing: taking something that belongs to someone else by force or secrecy and claiming it for your own.

What qualities or characteristics do children (and adults) need to be honest human beings?

In my school, whenever I encountered a child who had serious problems with cheating, stealing, or lying— and by serious I mean recurring and long-lasting episodes—I would ask myself what was missing. I concluded that three things were absolutely essential in a child if I (as a school principal) was going to have any impact on that child for the better. They were the ability to be empathetic; the ability to feel shame, sorrow, and remorse for the misdeed; and some shreds (however small they might be) of self-esteem or self-worth. Without at least one of these three, a child was in serious trouble. I rarely was succesful in helping a child to "get back on track," sometimes even with professional interventions (like counseling or therapy), if these important characteristics were missing.

My most challenging case involved a nine-year-old girl in third grade. Quiet and unassuming, she hardly created a ripple in the culture and climate of her classroom. No one, it seemed, was aware that she was even there. She never volunteered in class, had no friends, and "made no waves." Special teachers like the librarian, the art and music teachers, and the physical education teacher could scarcely remember her name, so skillful was she at disappearing into the woodwork. But she desperately wanted to be noticed and set about getting our attention in the only way she knew.

At first there were only a few complaints. Food was missing from students' bag lunches that were kept on wooden shelves above the coat racks outside the class-room. Students were frequently moving about the hallways on their way to the library, office, or special classes. So, my secretary and I theorized as we attempted to solve this problem, we will instruct the students to bring their lunches into the classroom with them, thereby removing the temptation from the culprit.

This plan seemed only to exacerbate the problem. A veritable committee of third graders appeared on my doorstep after lunch every day, listing the things that were missing from their lunches: Fritos, cupcakes, homemade cookies, and candy bars. Apparently our thief had discriminating taste. Only junk food was stolen.

I was becoming irritated at the amount of time this problem was consuming. There were no students in the third grade class who immediately came to mind as possible suspects, although I could think of several possibilities in the upper grades. I decided to be more systematic in my approach and set aside a morning to interview each third grader individually. I selected a newly sharpened pencil and a yellow legal tablet and instructed the teacher to send them down, one at a time, to talk with me. I seldom resorted to asking kids to "tattle" on their peers, but I was desperate. Parents were beginning to complain about the "stealing" at school, and I was beginning to look ineffectual as an administrator in their eyes.

As I talked with each student, looking for who might even have the opportunity to steal the food for so long without getting caught, the finger began to point in just one direction—Kimberly. She always seemed to linger behind when the rest of the class went out for recess. Or she found reasons and excuses to go back into the building (e.g., a forgotten jump rope, a misplaced mitten). Someone had seen her eating food on the playground at recess, but had never mentioned it to an adult before. The pieces began to fall into place.

Finally, after I had talked with everyone, I called Kimberly to my office to confront her. Although there were many sixth-grade boys who probably believed I had supernatural powers when it came to uncovering wrongdoing and persuading the perpetrators to "fess up," there was nothing magical about it at all. I just talked informally with boys and girls about how we feel when we've done something we know we shouldn't do—about concepts like guilt and shame. I always talked about the importance of "getting something off your chest," saying that when we've done something wrong we often feel like a giant weight is resting right where we breathe. I let them know that I was disappointed in their behavior, but I believed that if they genuinely felt sorry, we could start a new day together and both forget the misdeed. With most kids my methodology was almost foolproof. With Kimberly, I felt as though I'd been slammed into a brick wall. I was virtually certain that she had systematically stolen the food over a period of several months, but she would not admit to it.

We both took a break when she went to lunch, and I shared my frustration with my secretary, a wise woman and mother of two grown children. She was often my sounding board for difficult problems. She suggested that I not concentrate on getting Kimberly to admit to everything, but focus on just one piece of food from just one lunch bag. Her insight proved to be remarkable. Kimberly did admit to taking just one thing, but she never could bring herself to confess to the "whole crime." Usually as I talked with children about a wrongdoing, I would ask them to call their parents to tell them what had happened.

Even the most hardbitten sixth-grade boys would dissolve into tears at the prospect of telling their mother that they'd done something wrong and then lied about it. But Kimberly evidenced no shame or regret. She never shed a tear. My heart ached for her inability to experience the release that comes from confession and acceptance—the knowledge that I'll still be loved even though I've done something bad.

In the course of our discussion, I attempted to elicit from her some sense that she understood what the students in her class had been going through during the past months as day after day their lunch bags were violated and they had to look with suspicion on anybody in their class. Kimberly just didn't get it. Her own feelings of self-esteem and self-worth were non-existent. It was not one of my proudest moments as a principal. I referred Kimberly to the school counselor, but she transferred from our school before the year had ended. I still wonder about her.

How can the Bible, my church, and my faith help me raise honest kids in a dishonest world?

I often wonder how parents who are attempting to raise honest kids in our dishonest world do it *without* biblical principles, faith in God, and backup from dedicated clergy and committed Sunday school teachers and youth leaders. We need all the help we can get to combat and counterbalance the moral relativism that insidiously pervades our twentieth-century culture.

What do parents do who are unable to cling to the moral authority of God? How can families cope whose standards and expectations are constantly being redefined by popular notions of right and wrong? Without the Ten Commandments, the Golden Rule, and the Sermon on the Mount, we have little more than shifting sands on which to construct our children's virtues and values. To teach values in a vacuum, as so many popular books are attempting to do, is to deny the source and power of our Christian ethical framework. We are powerless to do it on our own.

Notes

1. *USA Today,* 23 February 1996, p. 1.

2. These figures come from Claudia H. Deutsch, "Students Cheating Even More," *New York Times,* repr. in *San Francisco Chronicle,* 15 April 1988, p. B3.

3. As reported in *Why Kids Lie; How Parents Can Encourage Truthfulness* by Paul Ekman (New York: Scribner's, 1989), p. 67.

4. Hugh Hartshorne and Mark May, *Studies in Deceit,* Book 1, "General Methods and Results," (New York: Columbia University), 1928.

5. Kraut and Price, "Machiavelliansim"; M. Lewis, "How Parental Attitudes Affect the Problems of Lying in Children," *Smith College Studies in Social Work* 1 (1931): 403-404.

6. Michael Schulman and Eva Mekler, *Bringing Up a Moral Child* (New York: Doubleday, 1994).

7. K. MacDonald, "Warmth as a Developmental Construct: An Evolutionary Analysis," *Child Development* 63 (1992): 753-773.

B. Weiss, K. Dodge, J. E. Bates, and G. D. Pettit, "Some Consequences of Early Harsh Discipline: Child Aggression and a

Maladaptive Social Information Processing Style," *Child Development* 63 (1992): 1321-1335.

8. John White, *Parents in Pain* (Downers Grove, Ill.: InterVarsity Press, 1979).

9. L. J. Severy and K. E. Davis, "Helping Behavior among Normal and Retarded Children," *Child Development* 42 (1971): 1017-1031.

F. F. Strayer; S. Wareing; and J. P. Rushton; "Social Constraints on Naturally Occurring Preschool Altruism," *Ethology and Sociobiology* 1 (1979): 3-11.

N. Eisenberg-Berg, and C. Neal, "Children's Moral Reasoning about Their Own Spontaneous Prosocial Behavior," *Developmental Psychology* 15 (1979): 228-229.

2

Why Do Kids Lie, Cheat, and Steal, and What Can We Do?

Holly was a bright, energetic, and capable sixth grader. Her parents were older professionals, and although Holly was a tagalong child with an already grown sister, they were as much involved in the life of our elementary school now as they had been during their older daughter's attendance. They were PTO officers, attended every fun fair and musical concert, and were very supportive of me and the teaching staff. Holly was going to graduate at the top of her class and gave every evidence of being a "near-perfect" child. That is, until Miss Lemon arrived on the scene.

Hired to complete the last month of the school year for a teacher who had just delivered a baby, Miss Lemon seemed to bring out the worst in Holly.

Whether the blame could be laid on a personality conflict, adolescent hormones, or a power struggle that would rival any in the corporate world, Miss Lemon and Holly went at it like two quarreling alley cats. Of course Miss Lemon's immature behavior only fueled the fires of Holly's passionate distaste for the teacher, but my problem remained one of keeping both of them on an even keel for the final two weeks of the school year. During those two weeks, Holly got into all kinds of trouble. And she continued to lie about exactly what was happening.

I was caught between a rock and a very hard place. Her parents couldn't believe that Holly was behaving in this way, and I somehow had to hold Holly accountable for her behavior while remediating an unfortunate employment decision in the person of Miss Lemon. I spent several sleepless nights figuring out why Holly, a seemingly polite, well-mannered, and respectful child, had turned into a manipulative liar overnight.

Lying

There are several common reasons children lie, and I could have put my finger on several of them in Holly's case: She wanted to demonstrate her power over this new authority figure; she wanted to avoid getting punished for doing some rather silly and immature things; she wanted to protect her friends in the class from getting into trouble; and she was clearly enjoying the admiration and interest of the other students in the class.

Holly just needed a good dose of reality, and fortunately her parents were clear-headed and sensible people who were able to step back and see exactly what was happening. Although their first reaction was to turn on the teacher, the school, and me, their good judgment and maturity prevailed, and we were able to put everyone back on track. Holly went on to middle school, no doubt blushing with embarrassment from time to time as she remembered her youthful brush with dishonesty.

Understanding the possible reasons children may lie will help you handle those periodic episodes that occur with calmness, wisdom, and common sense.

How should I deal with a child who has lied to me or to others?

1. Accept and confront the fact that your child has told a lie. Sometimes we're tempted to overlook a tall tale told by a preschooler, but it's best to always use a healthy dose of reality to counter the fantasy life of the very young child. For example, "That's a wonderful story, but I'd like to know the real reason you're covered with mud." Point out the differences between fairy tales, fiction, and fact as you read aloud to your children.

As you examine the severity of the situation that precipitated the lie, ask the following questions:

- Did your child make a choice to do something deliberately that she knew you believe is wrong?
- Was any harm done? Was anyone hurt? Was property damaged?
- Did lying make the situation even worse than it was?

- Was the lie told to cover up something he did that was illegal or immoral, or was the lie told to cover up breaking a household rule (curfew, homework, friends, chores)?
- Was the lie premeditated? Planning ahead to skip school for the day and concocting a story to explain your absence to school officials is definitely a premeditated lie. In criminal law, premeditation calls for more severe punishment.

2. Try to determine the reason your child lied. Once you know the circumstances, you can better deal with the incident. I have always been more lenient regarding consequences with a student who is forthright and honest about her transgression and mature about accepting the consequences. Later in this chapter we look at the specific reasons kids lie and how you can respond.

3. Consider your child's age and maturity level when dealing with a lie. The consequences and treatment of a lie told by a three-year-old who broke a sibling's toy by accident will be far different than those for a teenager who broke curfew, drove to another state with friends, and lied about where he was and what he was doing.

4. Don't consider the act of lying more important than the infraction behind it if your child is lying to cover up some serious misdeed.

Why do children lie, and how can we respond?
Your assignment as a parent is to examine the following list of possible reasons and determine which

among them might be behind your child's lying. Then, in addition to dealing with the specific episode of lying, you should also take steps to remediate any problems that may have precipitated the lying (See chapter 4).

To gain attention by spinning yarns and/or creating fantasy. Some children have vivid imaginations and construct elaborate tales that, while not lying in the strictest sense, may lead to lying if your child learns to get attention from parents and other adults in this way. While "making up stories" that are colorful and creative is certainly not lying by our definition, encourage your child to understand the difference between fantasy and reality. Confusing reality and fantasy is a part of your child's development. *It should not be punished.* Just keep in mind your child's maturity and motivation. Always state matter-of-factly to the child that what she is saying is not the truth. Talk about the difference between make-believe and truth, and ask her to give you examples of both. For some particularly imaginative children this process may take some time, often until the age of five, six, or even seven. Don't be discouraged.

To boast. Another behavior that, while not always lying in the strictest sense of the word, can certainly lead in that direction, is boasting. Children make up exotic vacation trips, tell the class they are moving to faraway states, or brag of knowing television stars or sports heroes—all to impress their friends and bolster their sense of self-importance. Sometimes what appears to be a childish boast is the truth. One third grader's father drove a limo, and he was always picking up somebody famous, but for most children, their boasts were an attempt to impress others and gain social status.

If your child has this tendency, you may need to bolster your child's self-esteem. If he feels the necessity to lie to feel good, there's something missing. Spend more time with your child, catch him being good, and find ways to affirm how special and unique he is.

To avoid punishment. The most common reason that children lie is to avoid punishment. Although parents glibly assure their offspring that "I'm more upset with your lying than with what you actually did [break my Waterford crystal, tip over a glass of chocolate milk in the refrigerator, decorate the bedroom wall with grafitti]," kids don't seem to have much faith in what their parents are saying. Their immediate reaction upon being accused is similar to that of Adam and Eve in the Garden of Eden: "Who, me?" Lying in self-defense to get out of a predicament is an age-old, knee-jerk response. Some parents believe that the real problem is the initial act of disobedience. They view the lie as a natural act of self-protection.

To respond to these sorts of lies, examine the kinds of consequences you've been handing out for misdeeds. If your punishments are harsh and unjust (even for minor problems), you're making it more attractive to lie than to face up to what you're going to mete out.

Gain for oneself. Some children lie to get something they couldn't get any other way. Young Raymond in chapter 1 would not have been able to get the pennies he needed for his cap pistol without lying to his mother. We love the story, but the truth is, he lied to get what he desperately wanted. There was no other way for him to reach his desired goal.

Children who lie to get something for themselves often need help in problem solving. Explore with your child other ways he might have of getting what he wants.

To cover up breaking a rule. Lying is sometimes the symptom of a more basic difficulty—your child's unwillingness to accept the rules that have been established. This kind of lying is frequently observed in adolescents. They feel that the family rules about curfew or about where and with whom they may drive the car are unreasonable. Therefore, they feel quite justified in lying to you about breaking the rule or the curfew.

The best remedy for this kind of lying is to develop the rules collaboratively (e.g., in a family council) and then get your child to agree that the rules are reasonable and that he has an obligation to obey them. When rules are arbitrary, capricious, and totally imposed by a parental or educational authority figure, there's a good chance that kids will test the limits and break them. Without cooperation, the only way to get your child to follow rules and tell the truth might be to keep the threat of punishment constantly hanging overhead. This means that a child does not buy into the rules but simply keeps the rules until he or she moves out of the family home.

Out of loyalty. Another common reason for lying is to protect friends. When their friends are in trouble, many children feel duty-bound to protect them. Educators and parents can sometimes unwittingly create a monster when they tell children on the one hand "not to tattle," but insist on the other hand that their children inform on siblings and friends when some-thing serious has happened. This conflict that every child experiences more than once during the growing-up years is a difficult one. Where does my loyalty to friends stop and my responsibility to my teacher and parents begin?

This is one of the most difficult lies to handle. We want our children to be loyal and trustworthy, but we also want them to realize the consequence of covering up actions that are illegal, immoral, or dangerous. Harsh or punitive consequences for this kind of lie will be very counterproductive. Before you back your child into the proverbial corner to "tattle" on someone else, see if you can gather facts from other sources to flesh out what really happened.

To avoid embarassment. When a child has been caught in a social faux pas (wetting one's pants ranks high on the list of social faux pas in elementary school), you can usually bet on his lying about it if you ask. I generally never demanded that a child testify against himself in such an embarassing situation. I just stated the facts: "Looks like you had a little accident. Nothing to worry about. We'll have some clean clothes for you right away." As children get older, there are innumerable social situations in which they may feel trapped into lying to avoid embarrassment in front of friends. I've fallen into this trap on many occasions in an effort to disguise personal weaknesses or errors in judgment. If a child is continually lying to cover embarrassment, work to build her social skills and self-esteem. Help her understand that eve-ryone makes mistakes or social errors, and it's okay to be imperfect.

Withholding information. When a peer or sibling is doing something potentially harmful, the withholding of that information from the proper authorities is a lie. If a child knows that a sibling or peer is dealing drugs, driving under the influence, involved in a destructive sexual relationship or any type of illegal activity, that child has a responsibility to share that information.

This lie is similar to that told to cover for a friend or because a rule is considered unfair. Open the lines of communication and build trust so that your child will find it natural to talk over with you situations involving friends who are making very bad errors in judgment.

To protect privacy. I've included this reason for lying, although it is more frequently used by adults than by children. Children sometimes overhear parents discussing job changes, having arguments, or even engaging in sexual intercourse. Rather than either telling the truth or telling children that the matters they may have overheard are private, parents may fabricate stories that only serve to confuse children. Children may follow suit by lying about private matters when they are of an age to not want their parents to know all about their activities and behaviors.

Children, especially adolescents, may have an unrealistic view of what is "private" in their lives and what their parents have a right to know. Open discussion with children as they mature about what parents have an obligation to know may head off problems with lying. One author offers the following checklist as examples of what parents have a right to know. Try discussing these with your children:

- Behavior of friends
- Whereabouts in free time
- Information about friends
- Behavior at parties
- Snacking behavior
- Television programs watched
- Homework accomplished
- Behavior at school
- Sexual behavior with peers
- Use of drugs
- Rides in cars with others
- Behavior driving the car.[1]

Some parents believe that a child's room is off limits and that reading material, letters, and telephone calls are private. Other parents believe that everything in their child's life should be an open book to them. It's important to talk about these things before problems arise.

For power. This reason for lying is often used by older children on younger children. The conversation may go something like this: "I'll give you the silver dollar I have in my bedroom if you'll take the garbage down to the curb for me." The gullible younger child dutifully takes the garbage down, only to have the older sibling tell him, "I was kidding." No, he wasn't kidding; he was lying. Bullies, braggarts, and playground troublemakers are master power liars. They use lies to maintain power over those who are weaker.

These are dangerous kinds of lies, often called Machiavellian, after Machiavelli's book *The Prince,* written in 1513. Machiavellian behavior is associated with "guile, deceit and opportunism in interpersonal relationships."[2] If your child is "Machiavellian" in nature, pay attention and get some help. We all know adults who are skilled and ruthless at getting what they want from others, lying effortlessly to achieve their goals. And I have encountered my fair share of children who rank among the best. Their behavior patterns are frightening.

One doesn't expect children to be so skilled at manipulating others (especially adults and parents). We cling to the myth that children are innocent. A number of landmark studies have been conducted with both children and adults to determine whether someone has Machiavellian characteristics and whether Machiavellian individuals lie more. Here are some sample items from a questionnaire given to children to determine whether they possessed "Mach" characteristics.

- Never tell anyone why you did something unless it will help you. (A Mach answers yes.)
- Most people are good and kind. (A Mach answers no.)
- You should always be honest, no matter what. (A Mach answers no.)
- It is better to tell someone why you want him to help you than to make up a good story to get him to do it. (A Mach answers no.)[3]

Forty-eight pairs of fifth graders were given the entire questionnaire and based on their scores were labeled high-Mach, middle-Mach, or low-Mach. The labels described their propensity for Machiavellian behavior. Middle-Mach children were then paired with high- and low-Mach children.

The pairs of children were invited to an interview room where the middle-Mach child was told to read a magazine while the other child was taken into a separate room. The interviewer explained to the child that she worked for a cracker company and her job was to find out what the child thought of a new cracker. The sample crackers were distasteful, having been contaminated by a quinine solution. The interviewer explained that she was having a real problem convincing anyone to buy the crackers since they obviously weren't very tasty. But since no one would even finish one cracker, they couldn't get a good idea of what was really wrong with the taste. She offered the child the opportunity to earn five cents per cracker if he or she could convince the partner, who was in an adjacent room reading a magazine, to eat some of the crackers. She explained that she didn't care what the child told the partner; the object was to get him or her to eat crackers. Then the pair was reunited and their conversation tape-recorded. Children who had scored high on the Mach test were more successful in getting their peers to eat the crackers than the low-Mach kids. How did they succeed? By lying.[4]

If your child shows signs of becoming a manipulative liar who will stop at nothing to get what she wants, examine the situation thoughtfully. Maybe it's just a passing stage. Talk with other adults who know your child well, like coaches, teachers, or youth workers. Listen carefully to their opinions. Examine your own behavior. Are you such a pushover that you are unwittingly encouraging this kind of behavior? Or are you a manipulator yourself who is providing the perfect role model for your child?

To build status. Where does telling a good story end and lying begin? As one who loves to tell stories about myself, my family members, and my work, I frequently fall into the trap of elaborating a bland story to win the interest or admiration of others. I must be constantly vigilant that I remain truthful to what actually happened. Of course, that temptation is even greater for children who may see tall tales as a way to gain the status they lack in size and age.

Handle status-building lies in a similar way to boastful lies.

To avoid an awkward social situation. This common reason kids (and adults) lie is similar to lying to avoid embarassment. Have you ever instructed a child to inform a caller that you aren't home? Have you fibbed to escape a social engagement with someone you didn't want to see? Have you told someone they looked ravishing when they obviously have been ill? These "little white lies" are used by children because they see grownups using them all the time.

Adults provide wonderful role models for their children in telling this kind of lie. Aunt Mary and Uncle George invite us for a holiday dinner and we plot around the dinner table about how to avoid it. The boss calls and asks to speak to Dad, who instructs young Billy to say he isn't home. It's impossible to tell your kids not to lie if they see you doing it. No one ever said that parenting would be easy. Take the beam out of your own eye before you ground your child for a week because of a speck in his eye.

Of course, there are good reasons for instructing children *not* to reveal that they are home alone when they, in fact, are. Ideally, perhaps you can come up with a solution that will avoid revealing the truth without lying. Simply saying, "He's unavailable right now but can call you back very soon if you leave a message" might do the trick. But a nosy caller may ask for details that will force a child to lie or admit she is home alone. Try explaining to your child that there may be a limited number of situations where lying is a better choice than risking personal safety. Life is full of ethical dilemmas, and sometimes our choice is between the lesser of evils. Children have to learn that eventually, and they can usually do so without compromising their basic honesty.

Stealing

Nothing strikes terror in a parent's heart like getting a phone call from the convenience store with the news that a child has been caught shoplifting. Nothing makes a teacher feel more violated than to discover that money is missing from the purse that was carelessly left on a classroom desk.

How can we respond?

If your child has problems with stealing, it will be important for you to have the child (1) return the item that was stolen to the person it was taken from, (2) apologize to the person, and (3) do something in the way of restitutiton for causing trouble and betraying a trust. I have found in my experience as an elementary school principal that nothing caused more anxiety and distress in a teacher than discovering that a child had stolen something from her. The sense of violation and betrayal was immense, and the resultant anger was frequently intense. Perfectly reasonable and sensible educators often demanded retribution that would have made the caning in Singapore seem humane. I share this information with you to emphasize how important restitution and apology are when you find that your child has stolen something.

It is painful for us as parents to experience this with our children, but if they don't experience shame, discomfort, and embarassment, they may be strongly tempted to repeat the action. If a stolen item is very costly and it has been damaged, lost, or given to someone else, determine a repayment shedule that is reasonable. A child should be inconvenienced but not reduced to complete poverty by the repayment schedule. Don't force your child to steal again by taking all of his money.

If this is the first incidence of stealing, mete out the consequences. Punishment should be swift and consistent, but there's nothing wrong with sending a child to his room for a period while you reflect on exactly how to handle the situation. In my experience, giving a child a little time to "sweat it out" adds to the effectiveness of the consequences. They may imagine something far worse than that which actually comes to pass, and there's nothing wrong with that at all.

Don't be tempted to reduce or eliminate consequences in the face of tears, abject apologies, explanations, and promises. No matter how sorry the child is, the consequences must be firm.

Try to determine the reason your child has stolen. Once you know the circumstances, you can develop a remediation plan to make sure your child does not steal again. The purpose of this investigation is not to excuse the stealing, but to find out what you need to do to make sure it won't happen again.

Try to learn your child's reasons for stealing and respond accordingly.

There are a variety of reasons children may steal, and most of them are easily remediable.

Confusion of borrowing and stealing. Younger children may have a difficult time telling the difference between borrowing and stealing. They will need instruction in the idea that taking something without asking is really stealing, even though they may be convinced that the person from whom they are taking it would be willing to loan it to them if he or she were available. Looking the other way when children continually borrow without asking can sometimes set an unfortunate precedent for widespread "borrowing." Likewise, young children may confuse finding and stealing. A child who has seen a sibling pick up and keep a quarter left on the sidewalk may find something in a store aisle and think that the same rule applies: If there is no owner, you can keep it. Explain that buying (paying for something with money, a check, or a credit card) is the only way to get something from a store.

Economic deprivation. Some children steal because they don't have money to buy the things they want. Whether this economic deprivation is real or imagined makes little difference—the outcome is the same.

Parents can help their child think of some other options he might have to get what he wants. Rather than stealing he could save allowance money, use Grandpa's birthday check, get a part-time job, or do extra chores around the house for money. Emphasize the importance of earning one's way, and then make sure your child has opportunities to do that. One young man I spoke with recently was bemoaning the fact that there weren't any chances to earn money at home anymore. His mom had hired a cleaning lady. A collector of pets, computer games, and other assorted memorabilia, this preadolescent could easily become frustrated and reason that he is justified in taking the things he needs.

To support a habit. The skyrocketing crime rate in some metropolitan areas is suggestive of an increasing number of petty burglaries in which young people are exchanging stolen goods for drugs. Neighbors in an affluent suburb in the Chicago area were shocked to find that a recent rash of burglaries had been committed by two high-school students who were using the proceeds to support their habits.

If your child is stealing because she needs money for drugs, the big problem is not stealing—it's the power that drugs have over her life. Get professional help immediately!

Emotional deprivation. The absence of parental love, attention, respect, or affection can sometimes be acted out in a child's life through stealing. There are numerous instances in which I've seen stealing begin after a parent has died or left home because of divorce or separation. The child is crying out for someone to notice him.

If your child is substituting things in his life for the warmth and love of a parent, it's time to rearrange your priorities. Divorce, death, new babies, and job transfers are all life-changing stressors that can divert our attention temporarily from children. If a child who has never been in trouble before is suddenly shoplifting or stealing money from your purse, "wake up and smell the coffee." This child is crying out for a little TLC.

Immaturity. A child may steal due to immaturity and the inability to delay gratification. Many parents have told a child *no* in the supermarket line only to have the child pick up the candy bar or pack of gum and carry it out of the store. Stealing incidents like this generally peak at around the ages of five to eight and decrease as the child matures and moral consciousness develops more fully.

A child who steals due to immaturity needs immediate consequences, solid teaching, and a good dose of love. Maturity will take care of this problem in the long run, but don't ever ignore it in the hope that it will disappear.

Desire for peer approval. Many gangs and informal groups of young people include stealing as a form of initiation into the group. An intense desire for peer approbation and the sense of belonging that comes from being part of a gang will entice many young people into stealing.

A child who is stealing to gain acceptance needs instruction in social skills and help in choosing and making appropriate friends. Work with school and church officials to get your child involved in positive, esteem-building activities.

Desire for revenge. Children who are angry with their parents, a teacher, or neighbor may try to get even by stealing something of value belonging to that individual. This thievery is a symptom of deep anger and resentment that the child feels powerless to address in more positive ways. Sometimes children, particularly adolescents, may want to embarass their parents in front of the community or church.

If your child is angry enough with you or someone else to steal from them, getting to the root of the problem is the most important issue at hand after dealing with the stealing itself. If necesary, ask an objective third party to mediate the conflict so that the child no longer feels the need to punish and retaliate.

To get attention. Some children steal things and all but leave a note telling you who did it. They seem to be begging to be caught, and indeed they are crying out for help with some problem. Depression, jealousy, anger, and rejection are emotional states that can cause children to act out by stealing. Look for these if your child is getting attention through stealing and you can uncover no other obvious problems. Then treat the jealousy, anger, or depression appropriately.

Following a poor role model. If an especially admired parent, friend, or sibling steals, a child can identify with this role model and steal as well. Carefully examine the influences in your child's life. If a family member who is dishonest lives with you, examine the effect this may be having on your children and take steps to separate that person from your children. If the poor role model is a custodial or noncustodial parent, get legal advice.

For excitement, risks, or thrills. Some children and young adults take great delight in living on the edge. The thrill of getting away with something and beating the system is a symptom of deep alienation between the individual, his family structure, and society.

If your child is stealing for the thrill, begin introducing field trips, family outings, and hobbies into your child's life. Keep her as busy and involved as possible.

To bolster self-esteem. If a child is unable to find an area where he/she can shine and be successful, that child may turn to socially unacceptable ways to bolster self-esteem. Showing off things they have stolen and bragging to peers about their machismo brings to them a form of prestige and acceptance they haven't found elsewhere.

You may find another book in this series, *Nobody Likes Me: Helping Your Child Make Friends,* a helpful resource for building social skills and self-esteem in your child.

Due to parental reinforcement and modeling. It's hard for most of us to believe that there are actually parents who gain vicarious pleasure from their child's misdoings. But I've had it happen. These parents are usually rebellious sorts who have always been at odds with "the system." They delight in the fact that their child is "showing them." These young people are unfortunately among the ones whose behavior may not always be remediable. The lifestyles and role models found in homes characterized by parental alcoholism, criminality, sexual abuse, and neglect exert an almost hypnotic effect on children, drawing them to lives riddled with antisocial acts and criminal behavior.

If you have a history of dishonesty, the likelihood of this problem showing up in your children is strong. Seek God's forgiveness and transforming power. Network with others who may have this problem to help you overcome your history. Get help immediately.

Cheating

Cheating is rampant in our world. The headlines are full of it. Politicians, sports figures, even religious leaders do it. People cheat on their income tax, cheat on their spouses, and cheat on the golf course. Children have so many prominent and visible role models who cheat that it's a wonder they don't cheat more often than they do.

What should I do if my child is cheating?
If you have discovered that your child is cheating, first think about possible reasons. Reasons are not excuses—to excuse the behavior would be a mistake. But you do need to determine why the cheating happened so you can take steps to make sure it doesn't happen again. Ask yourself the following questions:

- Am I unrealistic in my expectations or demands of my child? Do I continually emphasize the importance of winning or having top grades?
- Are my expectations far greater than my child could be expected to achieve (e.g., expecting someone who isn't physically coordinated to earn a place in the starting lineup or expecting someone with average ability to win a scholarship to Harvard)?

- Is my discipline so harsh and punitive that it engenders extreme fear in my children so that they cheat rather than face the consequences of failure?

Why did my child cheat?

Here are some of the main reasons children cheat and what you can do about them.

Competition and pressure. We want our kids to be number one—in academics, in sports, and in life. This intense pressure to be at the top of the heap engenders a "win at any cost" mentality that is very dangerous. Children who cheat have a much stronger need for adult approval than noncheaters do.[5] While high expectations are important, unreasonably high expectations can push children to be dishonest in the achievement of their goals.

If, after talking to your child's teacher, you determine that competition and pressure might be the reasons for cheating, lighten up. Major on praise and encouragement, rather than pressure. Avoid making comparisons between your child and siblings or friends with regard to report cards, sports achievements, or other accomplishments.

Feelings of inadequacy and unpreparedness. I must confess that if I was ever tempted to cheat on a test, it was when I faced Mr. DeWitt's math tests in high school. No matter how I studied or prepared, there was always a feeling of inadequacy. Fortunately, there were several roadblocks to this temptation—my parents, God, and the fact that Mr. DeWitt patrolled the aisles with an eagle eye. But I've empathized with many a student whose parents expected As when they were only capable of delivering Cs. Their own feelings of inadequacy and need for parental affirmation pushed them over the line.

If your child feels unprepared, offer to help your child study for tests. You might teach him some of the study strategies and test-taking skills in a companion volume in this series, *The Dog Ate It: Conquering Homework Hassles*. Solicit advice from your child's teachers if she needs extra help in the classroom.

To be numero uno. This is the child who is naturally aggressive and needs to be first at everything (especially games and sports). He has an inordinate need to win, and if it takes cheating, he may even do that. The child who needs to be number one may need constant coaching and nurturing to become less competitive and more forgiving of his own deficiencies. The impulsive, challenging child may need special help in this area.

Copy cat. Sometimes a younger child may see an older or more manipulative child cheat and win. She mistakenly assumes that this is the way "the game is played," and she lacks the maturity to realize the ultimate problems that cheating involves. Teach this child that cheating is wrong, and help her to understand that just because someone else does it, that doesn't make it right.

Laissez faire. Some parents are loath to come down too hard on their children, so they forgive a little "harmless fudging." They may even encourage it by doing homework for a child. Children are quick learners and will get the impression that a parent doesn't really care if they cheat. Before you know it, habits will be formed.

Cheating is not a problem that will disappear with age. It will only grow worse. Don't ever let a child get away with cheating. If you do, he will come to believe that nobody cares.

Egocentricity. This is a younger version of "numero uno." The young child firmly believes that he is the center of the universe and demands to be first and best, and to win at everything. In a mistaken attempt to make a child feel good, parents often unwittingly create a monster—a child who believes he can have what he wants, no matter what the cost. Deal with this problem as you would deal with the "copy cat" by teaching firmly and clearly that cheating is not allowed.

These are the reasons that kids cheat. If you can step back from the emotionally charged reaction you had when you first discovered that your little angel's halo was a mite tarnished, you'll probably be able to make some adjustments, fine-tune your parenting, and move into a proactive program to deal with the problem. The following chapter will give you some suggestions for how you can stop the problems before they get started.

Endnotes

1. Paul Ekman, *Why Kids Lie: How Parents Can Encourage Truthfulness* (New York: Scribner's, 1989), p. 123.

2. Richard Christie and Florence L. Geis, *Studies in Machiavellianism* (New York: Academic Press, 1970), p. 1.

3. Michael Korda, *Power* (New York: Random House, 1975), p. 327.

4. Dorothea D. Braginsky, "Machiavellianism and Manipulative Interpersonal Behavior in Children," *Journal of Experimental So-*

cial Psychology 6 (1970): 77-99. Note that this study did not use the Mach scale from which the examples were taken.

5. L. S. Dickstein, et. al., "Cheating and the Fear of Negative Evaluation," *Bulletin of the Psychonomic Society* 10 (1966): 319-20.

3

Parenting for Prevention

The demands of earning a living, managing a home, and parenting children are almost overwhelming as we approach the twenty-first century. We have fewer familial resources to fall back upon; grandparents are frequently living the good life in warmer climates. We have more stressful jobs; corporations are downsizing, restructuring, and reorganizing. And the expectations for increased productivity are everywhere: home, school, and work. Further, the influence of family and church in the lives of young people is diminishing.

In the sixties, the family was the most important influence in the life of children and young adults, followed by the school, friends, and the church—in that order. In the eighties the order of influence shifted, with friends superceding family as the number-one influence, followed by media and school. The church vanished altogether from the list as an influence in the lives of youth. Today, in the nineties, media tops the list as an influencer of youth—followed by friends, family, and the school. Families are losing ground with each passing decade, and the church has seemingly been buried.[1]

I fear that many parents simply aren't taking the time to listen to their children's cries for help and understanding. They are overlooking some basic and important principles of parenting that serve as a foundation for teaching the lessons of honesty and integrity. Listen carefully to the six requests your children are making of you each and every day. Oh, they may not repeat these exact words or even speak them aloud, but they come from the heart of each child.

In some families, children have become weary of making the requests and have turned to acting out for attention in ways like lying, cheating, and stealing. These behaviors are often cries for help and desperate pleas for parental attention. What are children telling us?

"Let me be me"

When my daughter was about three years old, I had my first inkling of what life was going to be about with Emily. She was due to wake up from her nap, and the room was suspiciously quiet. I went in to find her busily engaged in an art project with her new set of magic markers. She was carefully drawing designs at regular intervals on the white silk shade that graced her night table lamp.

I was aghast at such willful destruction. With the typical parental response, I raised my voice not a little and inquired, "Why in the world would you ever do something like that?" She didn't deny she was the culprit, but she seemed puzzled by my being upset. She calmly replied, "It was so dull."

Of course Emily was disciplined for her misbehavior. But I also began to understand what kind of child Emily was. She needed color, beauty, and art as a part of her regular environment. She needed paper, materials, and a place to work. She needed to be provided with opportunities to learn about different kinds of media. She was saying to me, in her own three-year-old way, "Let me be me! I'm an artist! Don't you understand?"

I'm certainly not condoning an environment that allows children to do whatever they want—we've always had rules and limits in our home—but I am suggesting that we be sensitive to who our childen are, and that we nurture and affirm that inner individual within the limits of our family.

"Spend time with me"

The demands of working parents and active families have created a dinosaur—the family dinner hour. The family that shares an evening meal regularly is fast becoming extinct.

Family members seem to have fewer and fewer opportunities to spend time together. Swimming lessons, tennis team, karate, art club, jobs, out-of-town trips, Awana, Pioneer Girls, church council meetings, Boy Scouts—you have your own list of things that conspire to keep your family apart. Don't let them. Make sure you build in lots of time to just be together. You can't suddenly launch into deep and meaningful discussions with your children when they become teenagers if you haven't talked along the way about the little things.

We worked at it during the years our children were growing up—the dinner hour was sacred. No one read books or newspapers. No one watched TV. We talked to each other. Everyone had to share the funny, frustrating, unusual, rewarding, or irritating things that had happened to them during the day. We learned about each other through these dinner conversations. If there were problems or unresolved issues, they usually emerged as we talked around the dinner table.

We need to spend time with the people we love! Especially our children. "Spend time with me" is the cry of children everywhere.

"Listen to me"

I sometimes have a problem with this third request, due to my constant "agenda anxiety." When people—whether my children, my husband, or my colleagues—start talking problems, my managerial and administrative juices begin flowing. I want to jump in and solve things. I have a hard time just listening and realizing that my family is not looking for "superwoman" to solve their problems. They are looking for a sympathetic ear.

With God's help, I'm learning to wait. I'm learning to hold back my will. I'm learning to listen to others. Knowing my propensity for jumping in and "making things right," my children would frequently caution me, "I just want you to listen, Mom. I don't want you to do anything about it."

Problems are healthy, and we can help children find ways to solve their own problems only when we listen well. Kids have a wonderful sixth sense that knows whether you're really tuned in and listening, or pre-occupied and just going through the motions. You have to learn to hang on every word. You have to learn to be interested in what your kids are interested in. Listen to them!

"Say no to me"

Children don't usually give verbal accolades to their parents when they lay down the law or give them the unvarnished truth about a situation. We need to have the wisdom and courage to know when and where the limits are appropriate. We pray for the Christian values we've instilled to bloom and flourish so that when we say no, our children will understand, agree, and obey.

Some parents can respond to all of the inner cries of their children except this one. They blow it on saying no. But we have to say no if we're going to succeed at parenting. Every situation must be dealt with individually, based on family rules and the maturity of the child. But be assured that if you haven't been saying no on a regular basis from your child's infancy, if you haven't been applying consistent biblical principles to your reasons for saying no, if you haven't respected your child as a person, saying no to a teenager will be a very difficult assignment.

"Support and encourage me"

As I looked at the hundreds of kids who came through the elementary school I served as principal, I could usually pick out those whose parents supported and encouraged them. Generally these kids did well in school, liked themselves, and got along well with teachers and fellow students. Their parents were interested in what their kids were doing. They allocated family resources to encourage hobbies, talents, and interests. They attended meetings, volunteered to be leaders, bought supplies and materials, and generally felt that the activities of childhood were worthwhile and important.

Now, there is a fine line between the "pushy parent," who is trying to realize his own unfulfilled dreams through his child, and the kind of parent who supports and encourages. I'm sure you know the difference.

In trying to be the positive kind of supporting and encouraging parent, I've supported a number of business ventures begun by my children. Few have been real money makers, but they've all taught valuable lessons and validated for the children that they are people, too.

One of our more interesting ventures involved fuzzies—those little yarn balls with faces and unique personalities. Some entrepreneur with more time and financial backing than we had has since put magnets on them, and now we see them everywhere. But when Emily and one of her friends went into the "fuzzy business" in third grade, it was unique.

She and a friend made up samples of some twenty different fuzzies, put them on display in the school library, and began to take orders. On the first day, more than thirty children placed orders for fuzzies. This venture naturally required a capital investment—yarn, felt, glue, and googly eyes.

As a parent, I had to make a decision—was I going to go out and buy seven different colors of yarn and fourteen different colors of felt, and drive to three different craft stores to find just the right variety of eyes? Was I willing to have yarn and felt scraps decorate the family room for the next two months? Was I willing to go through all of this knowing that since children are children, after a while their interest would wane and they would turn to some other activity? Of course I was!

How else do you encourage and support children? Let them know that their ideas are worthwhile? Validate them as unique human beings? You devote time and energy to their ideas and projects. You drive them to karate lessons because their participation will give them physical coordination and confidence in competition. You give them advice about starting up a lawn-mowing service over the summer and encourage them to follow through until the last leaf has fallen in November. You pay for music lessons and listen to them practice.

Our kids need to know that they can try and fail, and we will be there to help them try something else until they find their special niche.

"Let me go"

While we hold them tightly, our children are always straining against the parental bonds and saying, "Let me go." We let them go at many different stages. We let them go to school; we let them go to camp; we let them fly alone to visit Grandma; we let them go to college; and we give them our blessing as they choose a mate and marry. We let them go a little every time they try something new on their own.

Letting go requires faith that you have taught well. Letting go requires trust in your child. Letting go says, "I know you can do it on your own, but I'll always be here to help you if you have trouble." "Let me go" is one of the cries most difficult to respond to as a parent.

Letting your child go is one thing, but when she takes the family car with her, that's another. We experienced our first driving-related trauma soon after Emily received her license. Shortly after passing the driver's test, she asked to drive to an event near Chicago's O'Hare Field, the world's busiest airport. I wrote out the instructions carefully, much against my husband's better judgment. He felt she was too young, too inexperienced, too everything. We discussed the issue. My opinion prevailed. I hoped for the best.

It was a bright, sunny morning when she left. Her father lectured her on what to do if she got lost. "Don't panic," he stressed over and over. "Just be calm. You can always find your way if you don't panic."

I asked her to call when she arrived. About an hour after her departure, the phone rang.

Oh, good, I thought. *She's arrived safely.*

"Hi, Mom," Emily's voice rang out. "I think I'm lost. But I remembered what Dad said. I haven't panicked."

"Where are you?" I asked.

"A Shell station," she replied.

"Could you be more specific?"

"A Shell station at the corner of Damen and Blue Island."

Maybe she wasn't panicked, but I was. "That sounds like the south side of Chicago," I said, my voice rising, "You were heading for the northwest suburbs!"

"I think I made a wrong turn," she said. That was the understatement of the century.

Her father and I agreed that the best plan would be to have her get in the car, retrace her steps, and come home. I briefly described for her what she would have to do, and as our conversation was cut short by the operator asking for more money, I began to pray for her safe return.

I had to let go. I couldn't hold her on the phone and talk her home. She was on her own.

An hour later she drove into the driveway again. We both had learned from that experience.

If we listen to our children as they grow and mature, we will hear them saying to us: "Let me be me. Spend time with me. Listen to me. Say no to me. Support and encourage me. Let me go."

Our positive responses to these requests from our children will come back to us a thousandfold as we watch them grow and mature into children of honesty and integrity.

I hope you're already beginning to think about how you can change your family focus to respond to these heartfelt pleas from your children. There's more that you can do, however, to specifically encourage your children to tell the truth, respect the possessions and property of others, and abide by the rules. Implementing many or all of the following suggestions will help you to reorganize the priorities of your home and family, change your own behavior if needed, and make honesty a part of your family's mission.

How can I encourage my child to tell the truth?

The first and most important thing for any parent to do toward encouraging a child to be honest is to be a good role model. During these critical and impressionable years, be especially aware of your own white lies and what they communicate to your child. The temptation to exaggerate, fib, or tell a "little white lie" is always there, but guard your tongue most zealously against these traps. Bad habits like denying a mistake we've made, exaggerating an incident to make it more flattering, fibbing to escape a social engagement, or asking a child to inform Aunt Sally that you are not at home are lies that send the message to your children that it's okay to stretch the truth.

It is also important to avoid doling out punishment that is too severe or too frequent. Children who are terrified of overly strict punishments will often lie as a means of self-protection. Children who live in an environment of affirmation and praise will be more likely to admit they've done something wrong or made a mistake.

Consistently and intentionally teach honesty in your home. Let your children know in clear and direct ways that lying is wrong. Tell them that it demeans the liar, hurts those to whom the lie has been told, and is destructive of human trust and relationships. Be firm and unequivocal in your distaste for lying. It's okay for parents to do a little preaching and teaching. Don't be shy. Make honesty a part of your family's mission statement. Point out instances in which children and adults have been honest (e.g., finding money and returning it). Praise your children for being honest when you know it has been difficult for them.

How can I nurture in my child respect for the possessions of others?

Teach values in your home. If you are clear in communicating your values with regard to respect for the property and possessions of others, the likelihood that your child will have a serious problem with stealing is minimal.

Respect your child's right to personal property, and clearly establish property rights for all family members in your home. Explaining these rights and constantly teaching them to your children will sensitize them to the importance of respecting the property rights of others. For example:

- The person who owns an object has the right to determine who will use it and for how long.
- When you agree to let someone use something of yours, keep your word.
- Taking something that belongs to someone else, even if you're only intending to borrow it, is really stealing. Never "borrow" something from someone without first asking their permission.

These property rights will really be powerful if they apply to adults as well as children. This rule may take some discussion and negotiation around the family council to make sure everyone understands exactly how it works.

Make sure your child has the opportunity to earn money or have an allowance so she can buy some of the things she needs or wants. Encourage your children to come to you if they need money for a school or church activity.

Provide close supervision for your child. The more you know about where your child is going and with whom, the more likely you are to head off any possible problems. My son was spending some time with a couple of neighborhood boys who raised questions in my mind. Their principal form of entertainment was going downtown to wander around the stores. To me, this situation seemed ripe for problems. Although I trusted my son, I knew that in the company of these friends, he might well be tempted to "prove something." I didn't tell him he couldn't play with the boys, but I did ask him not to go to town. I was very frank in discussing my reasons, and he blessedly accepted my judgment and complied.

Remove temptation. None of us are above temptation. Leaving money where children may be tempted to "borrow" it is asking for trouble.

Give your child lots of opportunities for activities. Active, busy children are less likely to get into trouble.

Develop a close relationship with your child. Intimate parent/child relationships are the best antidote for any family problems. Children who feel close to their parents want to please them and are more likely to subscribe to parental values.

How can I help my child abide by rules and "play fair"?

Constantly teach moral values and lessons in your home. Emphasize the importance of personal integrity in being accepted and trusted by others. Explain that when you are dishonest, you are really cheating yourself as well.

Give your child affirmation and unconditional support. If your child believes that you will love him only if he gets all As or always wins at sports, his temptation to cheat will be much greater. Help your child to understand that practice and experience will bring greater skill and more winning opportunities. Share examples from your own life where you have wanted to win, but have lost fairly.

Be a good role model. Don't boast about speeding and not getting a ticket, the extra money you realized on a transaction because a sales clerk gave you the wrong change, or the fast one you pulled on the IRS by failing to report some extra income. You're inviting your child to follow in your footsteps.

Give a handicap. Bowlers and golfers are allowed handicaps all the time. They give a scoring advantage to those who lack the skill or experience to compete on an equal playing field. You can use this same technique to encourage and affirm your child. She may be far less likely to cheat given a fairer chance at winning.

Provide close supervision. Studies have shown that whenever children are left unsupervised during test taking or competitive games, cheating increases.

Build your child's self-esteem. (See chapter 4 for dozens of activities to build self-esteem and moral values).

But what do I do when I catch a child being dishonest?

We all know that children are going to lie, cheat, or steal. It happens. We can try to prevent it, but we also need to be prepared for it when it occurs. Let's summarize some guidelines for what to do when we're "on the spot"—having just discovered what our child has done.

Don'ts.

Don't ask your child whether she did it. Many parents confront a child who is probably guilty with a question which demands that the child testify against herself. But this is an open invitation to lying. If you already know the answer, confront the child with the facts rather than asking, "Did you do it?"

Don't ask your child why he did it. Children are dishonest for a whole host of reasons (see chapter 2), and the likelihood that he will be able to articulate the true "whys and wherefores" for you is very slim indeed.

Don't overreact and become angry and hostile. Screaming, shouting, and otherwise becoming hysterical won't help the situation or teach your child anything. Count to ten and take a calmer approach. The deed has been done. Clear thinking and reasonable problem solving should be the order of the day.

Don't be unwilling to listen to the truth. We often send messages to our children that we would rather not know the truth: "What you don't know doesn't hurt you." But in the case of our children, what we don't know hurts both us and our children. When we unwittingly or intentionally communicate to our children that we'd prefer to be left in the dark about the unpleasant or seamy side of their lives, we aid and abet them in lying and cheating. Be sure your demeanor is open, accepting, and forgiving. Your children will have far less reason to lie to you.

Don't administer corporal punishment. While I'm not totally opposed to corporal punishment, the kids and parents I've known for whom this was a common form of punishment never seemed to be doing too well. The kids were hostile; the parents were ineffective; and the results were disastrous. If the circumstances are right, the transgression very severe, and the child has not been spanked on a regular basis, a few well-administered placements of the hand can send the right message. But use caution, and *always* be calm.

Don't ground your child for the rest of his life. Don't overdo the consequences if your child has never had a problem before. Be fair, be firm, and then forget about it.

Don't brush the incident under the carpet. Sometimes parents are so embarassed by an incident of dishonesty, particularly if it involves the school or community, they just want to ignore it. Never overlook or minimize the problem. You're sending mixed messages to everyone if you do.

Don't defend your child. I've met with far too many parents who, rather than dealing with a problem of dishonesty squarely and letting their child know that what she has done is unacceptable, they make excuses and defend the behavior. "It was Johnny's fault, not my child's. You should have provided better supervision."

Blaming someone else for your child's dishonesty ranks right up there with suing the manufacturer of a ladder because you were putting up Christmas lights in the rain and fell off the top where you weren't supposed to be anyhow. Don't join society's trend to blame everyone else rather than accepting personal responsibility.

Don't treat your child like a criminal. Some parents begin to treat their children differently after an incident of dishonesty. They spy, they pry, they intimidate, and they totally lose faith in their children. Once a problem has been dealt with, wipe the slate clean. If God does it for us, we need to do it for our children.

Dos

What are the best ways to handle any episodes of lying, stealing, or cheating that happen at your house? Here are some things you *should* do no matter what:

Do communicate calmly and clearly that you will not tolerate dishonesty. Let your child know that if she is dishonest in the future, there will be consequences. Be creative in determining the consequences and if possible relate them to the dishonest action. Ask your child what you personally can do to help her with the problem.

Do help your child understand the natural consequences of lying, cheating, and stealing.

Ostracism, loss of reputation, and diminished trust and respect are all the natural fallout of being dishonest. A contemporary example of this principle at work is what has happened to O. J. Simpson. Although a jury of his peers found him innocent, the prevailing suspicion of guilt has taken away his status among his peers.

Do work in cooperation with teachers and administrators at school to solve the problem. If your child knows that there is an open line of communication between home and school, he will soon realize the futility of trying to cover up his inadequacies with regard to behavior and homework.

Do, once the consequences have been awarded, move on in a positive way. Be certain your child knows that you love her and that is the reason you are so concerned.

Do help your child get rid of his guilt. If your child does not have a severe behavior disorder or emotional problem, he will feel guilty. Feeling guilty when you've been caught and punished is normal and healthy. Feeling guilty forever, even when you've apologized, made restitution, and taken the punishment, is not healthy. Assure your child that God loves him and forgives him. Help your child to pray a prayer of confession and assure him of your forgiveness as well God's. If your child needs to ask forgiveness of a sibling, friend, teacher, or community member, help him to do that and then leave the problem in the past.

Do treat your child as a person of honesty and integrity, which she will become as she matures. Provide supervision, but don't treat your child like a criminal.

If your child has a pattern of frequent dishonesty, you should take it seriously and get professional help.

If you will remember these few simple dos and don'ts for dealing with dishonesty, you can turn what could have been a disaster into a positive learning experience for you and your child.

Endnote
1. From "The Teen Environment: A Study of Growth Strategies for Junior Achievement," Robert Johnston Co., Inc., 1980, p. 4, and discussion with Walt Mueller, president of the Center for Parent/Youth Understanding, Elizabethtown, PA.

4

Thirty-Five Thrilling Activities for Teaching Honesty

In 1983, syndicated columnist Dolores Curran surveyed 500 family professionals—teachers, doctors, pastors, Boy Scout and Girl Scout leaders, social workers, and others. This survey yielded fifteen qualities most often found in healthy families. I share them here, because the presence of these qualities in your home and family will do more than anything else you can do toward nurturing honest children.[1] The healthy family:

- communicates and listens to each other
- fosters table time and conversation
- teaches respect for each other

- develops a sense of trust
- has a sense of play and humor
- has a balance of interaction among members
- shares leisure time
- exhibits a sense of shared responsibility
- teaches a sense of right and wrong
- has a strong sense of family in which rituals and traditions abound
- has a shared religious core
- respects the privacy of one another
- values service to others
- admits and seeks help from others

The activities that follow will help build the healthy environment described in Curran's book. You'll have to set aside time, and that may require some realignment of your family priorities.

1. Be a Good Sport

We enjoy taking our grandchildren bowling and encourage them to support and cheer each other on. With the help of bumpers on either side of the lane, even the youngest is able to get an occasional strike or spare. The goal is not to get the highest score, which results in unhealthy competition, but to improve our own score from game to game. Your children will care about sportsmanship only if you teach them. The real goal of family sports and games should be self-improvement. Teach them that cheating, tantrums, fighting, and a "sour-grapes" attitude just aren't acceptable. Always talk about good sportsmanship before heading out to play.

2. Let's Make a Deal—Don't Steal

If your child steals something from a store, in addition to expecting her to apologize and return the item, Mark and Denise Weston suggest having the child do something for the store owner, like making a poster encouraging other children to be honest, or doing odd jobs.[2]

3. The Formal Apology

If your child has done something to hurt another person through lying, cheating, or stealing, have him write a note or design a card to send to that person. This is a particularly effective way to handle cheating and stealing at school. Gaining forgiveness from the person who has been "violated" is not always easy, and a formal apology may speed the process along.

4. The Fairy Tale Book

If your child has a problem distinguishing between fantasy and reality, make a Fairy Tale Book out of all the grandiose lies and long-winded stories your child tells. Explain that each story will be recorded, and that she can draw pictures of her stories for this special book. When you catch your child in an obvious lie, take out the Fairy Tale Book and say, "That's a good one. Let's write it in the Fairy Tale Book."[3]

5. Empathetic Listening

Empathy is one of the critical attributes needed by children as they mature in honesty and integrity. You can foster this quality in your children by engaging in empathetic listening when you talk with them. Empathetic listening means sending the message to the communicator that you understand their feelings and needs. This allows children to express their feelings without fear of being lectured or judged. It means listening with eyes, ears, heart, and soul. Try using statements like:

- "Sit down next to me and tell me why you're so upset."
- "I hear you saying that you think your teacher is unfair."
- "Sounds like you're too angry to talk about it right now."
- "I understand what you're saying, but I can't permit you to do that. It's not right."

6. The Honest Abe Award

Read about Abraham Lincoln and other historical figures whose lives were characterized by integrity and honesty. Institute an Honest Abe Award in your family. When you find tradespeople who do work for you, clerks in stores, family members, or friends who deserve the award, give them a certificate, a sticker, a pat on the back, or a compliment. If someone does something that's particularly outstanding, write a letter to the editor of the local newspaper commending their behavior.

7. Not As They Are, but As They Will Be

Treat your children not as they are, but as you hope they will become. This restatement of Dr. Haim Ginott's theory of child development has powerful implications for changing children's behavior. Although our children are born with different personality traits and temperaments, we as parents have the capacity to help them grow and change. We can help our children see their potential, and verbalizing our beliefs in their ability to be honest, kind, assertive, resourceful, and loving will be far more effective in bringing about change than constantly reinforcing a child's capacity for being a "thief" or a "liar." Our responsibility as parents is to help our children see and develop their potential strengths.

8. Fostering Empathy

Having empathy is critical to a child's ability to make honest choices. Here are some things you can do on an everyday basis to help your child develop empathy:[4]

- Draw your child's attention to people's feelings. Ask him to imagine how he would feel in the same situation.
- Let her know what the impact of her actions are on the feelings of others, including yourself.
- Explain why people feel the way they do.
- Make clear (or encourage him to discover) what actions he can take that would be more considerate.
- Let her know that you expect her to be considerate, that it is important to you.
- Let him know that you understand and care about his feelings, and try to offer him a way to get at least some of what he wants—if not now, then in the future.
- Don't expect her to read minds (yours or anyone else's). Take the time to explain.

- Help him understand other people's feelings by reminding him of similar experiences in his own life.
- Help her resist the influence of people who discourage or ridicule her empathetic feelings.
- Give him approval when he is considerate. Show disappointment when he isn't.
- Use empathy training to foster self-control; have her imagine herself in someone else's place whenever she is inclined to hurt that person.
- Share your own empathetic feelings with him.
- Point out examples of people who are empathetic and those who are not, and communicate your own admiration for kindhearted people.
- Stress the good feelings that come from caring about other people.
- Encourage her to consider a person's capacity for empathy when selecting friends.

9. Home Management System

Maybe you think that management systems are for large corporations and institutions. Think again. Your home could probably benefit from streamlining its management. Try this home management system, which has four parts:

- A *behavior management* plan is a set of rules and expectations for your child, and guidelines for what you will do and what will happen to him when the rules are not kept. The plan will govern how you discipline your child and how you respond to misbehavior.

■ A *problem-solving model* consists of a several-step process that parents can use with each other and children to identify and solve common problems. The model should be "practiced" and perfected using neutral dilemmas so that when genuine family problems arise, the skills are in place. Many families post the problem-solving steps on the refrigerator and refer to them during particularly tense situations, either for the child or for the family. One mother who occasionally "blows it" (as we all do) tries to model problem-solving behavior, thinking out loud about the choice she made, how it worked out, and what other choices she could have made.

■ Instruction for the child in *self-management* and self-instruction involves a set of skills and training for children that helps them develop an internal language of positive self-statements. This part of the home management system is particularly important if one of your children has a disability, is a challenging child, or has problems with self-esteem. This type of training is usually offered by counselors and psychologists, but you can help your children to use positive self-statements through modeling for them. "Talking to oneself" is something that adults do quite automatically. Children are not usually capable of self-instruction until the age of six or seven. Examples of positive self-statements that children might learn are

"I think I can do it"; "If I try, I can be successful"; "If I keep working, I'll improve."

■ A *family communication* model is the way that families regularly get together to talk about what is going on in their family (e.g., family council or family meeting).

A home management system will help family members relate to each other and help children learn the behaviors that smooth human relationships.

10. Communication

Effective and active listening is a very important part of solving relational problems, which is what lying, stealing, and cheating really are.

Listen to the content. Make sure you heard the words and ideas that the child is conveying to you.

Listen to the intent. Try to "hear between the lines." The emotional tone, pitch, and pace will often tell you more about what is being said than the actual words.

Be alert for nonverbal language. We often call this "body language." Gestures, facial expressions, and posture communicate just as powerfully as words.

Pay attention to your nonverbal language. If you're fidgeting or frowning, you could be communicating hostility toward or a lack of interest in what your child is saying to you.

Try to be empathetic and nonjudgmental. You can do this by trying to put yourself in another's position.

11. Problem Solving

Every family needs to have a way to solve the problems that arise from time to time, whether they be those that involve all family members or those between two or three family members. Here is a model that has worked well for me in many different settings:

Step 1: Begin to define the problem. Talk it over and write it down.

Step 2: Gather information. Get input from all of the people involved in the problem.

Step 3: Redefine the problem. The problem may be worse than you thought and have several aspects, or you may discover you really don't have a problem at all.

Step 4: Establish an acceptable outcome. Decide what you want to have happen as a result of solving the problem and if at all possible make the outcome measurable.

Step 5: Generate alternative means. Don't just settle for one solution to the problem; your first solution may not work.

Step 6: Establish the plan. Make sure you explain why the plan is being prepared, who is going to participate, what specific actions each individual will take, when these activities will be performed, and where they will occur.

A simpler plan that is more appropriate for children consists of the following steps:

Step 1: Stop! What is the problem I am having?

Step 2: What are some plans I could use?

Step 3: What is the best plan I could use?

Step 4: Do the plan.

Step 5: Did my plan work?

12. Walk a Mile in Another's Moccasins

Being able to understand how another family member may feel is an important skill for good family relationships and for success at school and in the "real world." Model, explain, and practice the following as needed in your family:

- Admitting that something is your fault (if it was) and saying you are sorry.
- Explaining your feelings about a situation.
- Attempting to see the other side of a disagreement.
- Being the first to "break the ice" if a grudge is prolonged.

13. Learning How to Apologize

Children need models for how to handle conflict. Integrate these statements in your family relationships and help your children to use them when appropriate.

- I never knew you felt that way.
- I didn't realize you would take it the way you did.
- I would have acted differently if I had known.
- I wish you had said something.
- I had no idea you were sensitive about the subject.
- I admit I was wrong. Can you forgive me?

14. Role-Playing

In role-playing, two or more individuals act out a brief scene from a hypothetical situation. If your child is having a problem making honest decisions, role-play with her so she can rehearse her behavior. Pose hypothetical situations for her so she can practice telling the truth and walking away from the temptations to cheat and steal.

15. Let's Talk about It

Small group discussion is an age-old methodology. It has been defined as face-to-face mutual interchange of ideas and opinions between members of a relatively small group. Your family is the original small group. Use a discussion process when the group has an idea, concern, or issue that is worthy of consideration. If you're not ready to try a regular family council, then everyone should at least talk about it once in a while. Make sure to have big sheets of paper for recording the "group memory." We used to have our group discussions in a restaurant that used white butcher paper for tablecloths. They furnished jars of crayons with which diners could write. We took notes on the "tablecloth," and that helped us keep track of our discussion. The leader of the group must model behaviors that are critical to the success of small group discussion.

- Encourage the expression of ideas by all members of the group.
- Establish and maintain an informal, cooperative, and open group climate.
- Make suggestions instead of giving directions.
- When necessary, bring in humor to enliven the atmosphere.

At the end of the meeting, summarize the results. If there are tasks or assignments to be completed, make sure they are written down and everyone agrees. This kind of open participation helps children feel that they have a say in family life, and that encourages honesty and responsibility.

16. Brainstorming

Brainstorming is a process in which a family group generates as many ideas or solutions as rapidly as they can without regard for immediate quality. The process can be random, where individuals call out ideas as they occur to them, or more formal and structured, where individuals write out ideas and are called on in turn to respond. Brainstorming is a good process to use when trying to solve a problem that may have many answers. Use a big sheet of paper and colored markers to record all of the suggestions. Here are the steps to follow:

- Clearly define and write out the question or problem for the group.
- List every idea as it is given, no matter how far out it seems to be. One idea per person at a time.
- Quantity is the goal. Quality will follow.
- Don't prejudge whether ideas are good or bad, just list them. Even silly ideas stimulate new, creative ones in yourself and others.
- No intimidation of group members with body language or verbiage.
- Don't explain your idea—be brief. Don't ask others for help in phrasing.
- Don't try to sell your idea—simply state it.
- No discussion or comments until after the list is complete.
- Don't repeat an idea, but you can add to one already listed.
- Work quickly.
- Invite everyone to participate, but don't force it.
- When the flow of responses stops, the process will be ended.
- Squeeze out the last possible idea; it might generate a whole new line of thinking.
- After all topics have been listed, allow time to review and/or clarify the topics.
- Brainstorming ideas must be evaluated and a process selected for determining which ideas will be considered in more depth or even used. Spending time on a brainstorming session without follow-up can be very bad for family morale.

17. S.T.A.R.

S.T.A.R. (Stop Think Act Right) is a "self talk" technique for children described in *Playful Parenting: Turning the Dilemma of Discipline into Fun and Games*.[5] If your children have a hard time exercising self-control, teach them how to use this technique when they feel the temptation to lie, cheat, or steal. First, your child will need to stop all activity and think rather than act. Once he has stopped (the proverbial count to ten always works well here), he needs to think about his options and make a decision about what to do next. S.T.A.R. spelled backwards is R.A.T.S. (Review Actions and Try Some more). Although this technique won't work with all children, the acronym will give you a simple way to remind your children to think before acting.

18. Catch Them Being Good

Many schools use this behavior model, and it works well on the home front as well. Make a batch of smiling and frowning faces on a sheet of $8\frac{1}{2}$ x 11" paper. Photocopy the sheet and cut them up. Whenever you "catch" your children making honest choices, toss a smiley face into a basket or box. Whenever your children are dishonest, put in a frowning face. At the end of a specified period of time, if there are more smiles than frowns, the family will do something special together like go out for pizza or go bowling. Take time before you begin this activity to make a list of all of the positive things that merit smiley faces and all of the negative things that deserve frowning faces.

19. Tell Me a Story

Look in the card catalog under the subject headings of *honesty* or *dishonesty*, and read about how some fictional characters cope with learning honesty and responsibility. There are dozens of good titles. Your library will have its own collection.

20. Self-Esteem Checklist

Could the problems with being honest at your house be the result of low self-esteem? Take a few minutes to assess your child according to the following lists. A child with high self-esteem will exhibit the following characteristics:

- is proud of her accomplishments
- can act independently
- assumes responsibility
- can tolerate frustration
- approaches challenges with enthusiasm
- feels capable of taking charge of situations in his own life
- has a good sense of humor
- has a sense of purpose
- can postpone gratification
- seeks help when needed
- is confident and resourceful
- is active and energetic
- spontaneously expresses own feelings
- is relaxed and can manage stress

A child with low self-esteem exhibits these characteristics:

- plays it safe by avoiding taking risks
- feels powerless
- becomes easily frustrated
- is overly sensitive
- constantly needs reassurance
- is easily influenced by others
- frequently uses the phrases "I don't know" or "I don't care"
- is withdrawn
- blames others for failures
- is isolated, has few friends, is preoccupied
- is uncooperative and angry
- is clingy, dependent
- is uncommunicative
- is constantly complaining
- has a general negative attitude[6]

If your child has low self-esteem, take steps to:

- build in more one-on-one time
- praise and affirm your child
- be a good listener
- practice being empathetic

Children who feel good about themselves will tell the truth and take responsibility for their actions.

21. Spare the Rod

The adage goes "Spare the rod and spoil the child." I prefer to think of the rod in a more figurative sense as an atmosphere of love and discipline in the home that fosters self-respect and cooperation. Discipline is always needed and very important, but I'm not certain that physical punishment achieves the desired ends if used more than just occasionally with small children. The publication *For Parents: A Newsletter for Family Enrichment* recently summarized these effects of spanking:

- Children who are often spanked tend to be more quiet, less articulate, and more sullen.
- Spanking tends to create nervousness and slow down learning.
- Harsh physical and psychological punishment leads to social distance among family members. When social distance increases, honest communication decreases.
- Frequent use of physical punishment is strongly associated with the development of a low self-image in children.
- Violence begets violence. Physical punishment for fighting does not teach kids to stop fighting.
- Spanking is related to chronic passivity in children.
- Children who are controlled through being spanked develop an overdependence on external control. They become followers, always dependent on the watchful eye of an overseer.

Have I ever been spanked? Yes. Have I ever spanked my children? Yes. Have I ever spanked a child in my school? No. But I supervised a father while he administered a paddling to his son. Do I recommend spanking as the *only* ammunition in your discipline arsenal? Never!

22. Put Yourself in the Picture

Be on the lookout for interesting scenarios or situations (involving honesty) as you travel, read newspapers, look at pictures, or overhear conversations. For example, a number of years ago in California, a visiting tourist from New Caledonia lost his wallet, containing close to twenty-five hundred dollars in cash, a credit card, passport, and plane ticket. These items were found by a couple and their eleven-year-old son, who at the time were homeless and jobless. They promptly turned everything in to the authorities. As a result of the news coverage received for what seemed to most like an extraordinary act of honesty, the family got contributions of more than sixteen thousand dollars from around the country. Stories like this one, although rare, give you an opportunity to discuss the concept of honesty and help to build empathy and understanding for the choices that others have made.

23. Family Devotions

These will never happen without a plan and commitment, but they are a critical and meaningful part of building family friendships. If you have memories from your childhood of interminable prayers and incomprehensible passages of Scripture, do some browsing at your Christian bookstore to find ideas for making your family devotions child-friendly.

24. Shared Values

There is nothing more destructive to family unity than dissonant values between husband and wife. Children are confused about just whose values are the most important. Take this little quiz separately, and then discuss the results and their implications for imparting values to your children.

1. It's okay to drive over 55 m.p.h. (or 65 or 75) even if that's the posted speed limit.
2. It's wrong to spank children.
3. It's okay to take ashtrays from restaurants or towels from motels—they expect it.
4. Padding the expense account is a reasonable response to unreasonable taxes.
5. It's okay to ask your children to tell "little white lies" about your availability for phone calls when you're actually present in the same room with them.
6. It's wrong to report on a neighbor if you see him doing something that's against the law.
7. Loyalty to friends is more important than telling the truth about something they have done.
8. There is no such thing as a socially acceptable lie.[7]

If your values differ dramatically, try to agree on what values to teach the children.

25. The Question

The chairperson (this assignment can rotate from meal to meal) asks each family member "The Question." The question can vary, but here are some examples:

- What is something you like about yourself?
- What is something you felt good about today?

- What is something you're happy about?
- What is something you're improving at?

26. Trust Building

Covenant with one another not to share information outside of the family that could potentially hurt another family member. Older brothers and sisters don't tell everyone that Johnny still wets the bed. Younger brothers and sisters learn to keep their mouths shut about Susie being grounded for violating curfew. Parents shouldn't tell amusing stories about their children, and spouses should be discrete about blabbing their mate's peculiar bathroom habits to the neighborhood. Don't share family failures with the world, and then your children will not be tempted to lie when confronted by a friend with embarrassing information.

27. It's Not What You Have but How You Got It

Teach your children to value hard work and productive efforts as opposed to possessions, wealth, top grades, or other visible evidences of achievement. This is a difficult value to affirm in today's society, where sports stars routinely make millions through intimidation, showmanship, and poor sportsmanship, and film and rock stars flout convention and morality on a daily basis. Discuss these issues in family chats. Make your views well known, and don't be afraid to bring them up over and over again for discussion. Your kids will "Oh, Mom or Dad . . ." you, but you have a responsibility to send a clear message about your family's values.

28. The Demonstration Game

Linda and Richard Eyre[8] suggest this game as a way to help small children grasp the terminology of truth and untruth. Ask them if they know the difference between something that's true and something that's not true. Start with simple physical facts, and then move to things relating to behavior.

- The sky is orange. (Kids say, "Not true.")
- (Point at foot) This is my foot. (Kids say, "True.")
- Ants are bigger than elephants.
- We see with our eyes.
- Milk comes from chickens.
- Take a cookie from the jar and eat it. Then say, "I didn't eat the cookie."

This exercise will help the youngest children begin to understand the different between truth and falsehood.

29. The Consequence Game

This game suggested by Linda and Richard Eyre[9] is designed to help children understand that the long-term consequences of honesty are always better than the long-term consequences of dishonesty. Prepare pairs of index cards. On one side of each of the cards in the pair, describe two alternative courses of action—one honest and one dishonest—along with the short-term consequences of each action. Fill out the other side of the cards so that when the two cards are flipped over, the long-term consequences are revealed. Play it as a game, letting children decide, by looking at the front sides only, which option they would take.

Front sides:

Option #1: You are at the store buying something and the clerk gives you $10 too much in change. You keep it. After all, it was his mistake and not yours. You go into the toy store next door and buy some new handle grips for your bike with the extra $10.

Option #2: When a clerk gives you an extra $10 in change, you tell him and give the $10 back. He says thank you, but as you walk out you think about the new handle grips for your bike that you could have gotten with the $10.

Reverse sides:

Option #1: You know the money wasn't yours. You start to worry that the clerk will have to pay the store the $10 out of his wages. Whenever you ride your bike, the new handle grips remind you that you were dishonest.

Option #2: You feel good and strong inside because you were honest. When you ride your bike, you remember that you don't have new handle grips but you were honest.

30. Dishonesty Brainstorm

This activity is particularly good for preteens and teens. Brainstorm all the different types of dishonesty that you can think of. Include dishonesty to parents, self, and peers, and dishonesty about activities, beliefs, and emotions. Encourage children to aspire to honesty even in the small matters where they might be tempted to tell "white lies."

31. Honesty Dilemmas

Share your own dilemmas with honesty. Be honest and relate instances in which you had a hard time and may have been dishonest. Having enough confidence in your children to share personal struggles will affirm your estimation of their maturity.

32. Scenario Game

The Eyres suggest devising a variety of scenarios (projected possibilities with consequences) and sharing them with your children. Here's one example. Others can be found in their excellent book *Teaching Your Children Values*.[10]

You're sitting in your English class, taking the final exam. You've studied hard, and the first two sections of the test are easy. The last section is much harder, and you realize it is from a book you forgot to review. You're pretty sure the teacher never told you to read that book. You feel mad at the teacher and that it's not your fault that you don't know the answer. The questions are multiple choice, and it's extremely easy to see Jim's answer across the aisle.

Discuss the consequences of making one choice or the other with your children.

33. True and False Loyalty Game

As an elementary principal, I spent lots of time trying to help kids see the difference between lying and keeping quiet to protect a friend. In one such instance three fifth graders skipped school and took the train thirty miles to Chicago. Only one child knew where they were and he wasn't budging on their location. I had three sets of frantic parents trying to locate their children, but a false sense of loyalty prevented him from telling on them. Help your children see the difference between loyalty and lying.

34. Short Rules to Live By

Give your children short rules to live by that you have indelibly imprinted on their minds by constant repetition. The Golden Rule, The Ten Commandments, Benjamin Franklin, and your grandmother are good sources to start with for these rules. Encourage your children to memorize Scripture. The biblical injunction to hide God's Word in our hearts so that we might not sin is a powerful tool to guard your children against dishonesty.

35. Be Truthful with Your Children

There's nothing more frustrating for a child than to ask parents for an explanation about something and be told "Because I said so, that's why." Whenever possible, give children truthful explanations for your rules and decisions. If you cannot give logical, well-reasoned answers, then perhaps you're being arbitrary and capricious.

I hope that as you've read this book you have gained some insight into why children sometimes behave in dishonest ways. And hopefully you have also achieved a measure of confidence in your ability to handle positively and productively any dishonesty you encounter. But more important, I hope that you have determined to make some changes in the way you "do business" in your family. As you work to build a healthy and honest family, remember the fifteen characteristics of a healthy family that we mentioned at the beginning of the chapter. Affix them to your refrigerator, write them on your heart, and practice them on a daily basis. They are your best antidote to dishonesty and your best insurance policy for a family whose children are characterized by integrity.

Endnotes

1. Dolores Curran, *Traits of a Healthy Family* (New York: Ballantine Books, 1983).

2. Denise Chapman Weston and Mark S. Weston, *Playful Parenting: Turning the Dilemma of Discipline into Fun and Games* (New York: G.P. Putnam's Sons, 1993), p. 73.

3. Ibid., p. 81.

4. Michael Schulman, and Eva Mekler, *Bringing Up a Moral Child* (New York: Doubleday, 1994), pp. 75-76.

5. Weston, p. 29.

6. Adapted from Harris Clemes, and Reynold Bean, *Self-Esteem: The Key to Your Child's Well Being* (New York: Putnam, 1981).

7. Adapted from Dolores Curran, *Traits of a Healthy Family* (New York: Ballantine Books, 1983), p. 215.

8. Linda and Richard Eyre, *Teaching Your Children Values* (New York: Simon & Schuster, 1993), p. 43.

9. Ibid., pp. 45-46.

10. Ibid., pp. 54-55.

Resources

Bennett, William. *The Book of Virtues.* New York: Simon & Schuster, 1993.

Briggs, Dorothy Corkille. *Your Child's Self-Esteem: The Key to His Life.* Garden City, N.Y.: Doubleday, 1970.

Curran, Dolores. *Traits of a Healthy Family.* New York: Ballantine Books, 1983.

Damon, William. *The Moral Child: Nurturing Children's Natural Moral Growth.* New York: Macmillan, 1988.

Ekman, Paul; Ekman, Mary Ann Mason; and Ekman, Tom. *Why Kids Lie: How Parents Can Encourage Truthfulness.* New York: Scribner's, 1989.

Eyre, Linda, and Eyre, Richard. *Teaching Your Children Values.* New York: Simon & Schuster, 1993.

Garber, Stephen, and Garber, Marianne. *Good Behavior: Over 1200 Solutions to Your Child's Problems from Birth to Age 12.* New York: Villar, 1987.

Garlett, Marti Watson. *Kids with Character.* Portland, Ore.: Multonomah, 1989.

Lickona, Thomas. *Raising Good Children.* New York: Bantam Books, 1983.

McEwan, Elaine K. *"Nobody Likes Me": Helping Your Child Make Friends."* Wheaton, Ill.: Harold Shaw, 1996.

Reuben, Steven Carr. *Raising Ethical Children.* Rocklin, Calif.: Prima Publishing, 1994.

Schulman, Michael, and Mekler, Eva. *Bringing Up a Moral Child: A New Approach for Teaching Your Child to Be Kind, Just, and Responsible.* New York: Doubleday, 1994.

Unell, Barbara C., and Wyckoff, Jerry L. *20 Teachable Virtues.* New York: Berkley Publishing, 1995.

Weston, Denise, and Weston, Mark. *Playful Parenting: Turning the Dilemma of Discipline into Fun and Games.* New York: Putnam's, 1993.